CATECHIST magazine's
prayers for
Catechists

Kass Dotterweich

Pflaum Publishing Group
Dayton, OH

CATECHIST® magazine's *Prayers for Catechists*

Cover and Interior Design: Kathryn Cole
Editor: Karen Cannizzo
Photos: Copyright © istockphoto.com: scorpio1811, vbice, maegg, BWBImages, and stuartkey

© 2006 Pflaum Publishing Group. All rights reserved. No portion of this text may be reproduced in any way or for any use without the written permission of the publisher.

CATECHIST® *is a registered trademark of Peter Li, Inc.*

Pflaum Publishing Group
2621 Dryden Road, Suite 300
Dayton, OH 45439
800-543-4383
www.pflaum.com

ISBN 978-1-933178-39-4

Table of Contents

Introduction 6
My Prayer to the Holy Spirit 7
My Morning Prayer 9

Prayer Before Planning a Lesson 10
Lesson Plan Blessing 11
Prayer Before Class 12

Prayer for My Students 13
Prayer for Special Needs of a Student 14
Prayer for Special Classroom Needs 15
Prayer for My Students' Families 17
Prayer with My Students 18

Prayer After Class 19
Prayer of Gratitude 20

Prayer to Share with Other Catechists 21
Prayer for Our Faith Formation Team 22
Prayer for Our Religious Education Program 23
Prayer for Our Parish 25

Prayer When I'm Lacking Confidence 26
Prayer When I'm Feeling Unappreciated 27
Prayer When I'm Feeling Burnout 28

A Catechist's Divine Praises 29
My Evening Prayer 31

Introduction

Along the Sea of Tiberias, the risen Jesus told his disciples where to cast their fishing nets for an abundant catch. He also prepared and served them breakfast (John 21:4-13). Oh how we would welcome clear directions in life—and someone serving us breakfast.

As catechists, we are Jesus' disciples today. May these short and simple prayers help us pause along the shores of our busy day, hear Jesus' gentle and directing voice, and feel nurtured and sustained in his presence.

—Kass Dotterweich

Editor, **CATECHIST**

My Prayer to the Holy Spirit

Come Holy Spirit,

> *guide and inspire me*
>
> *as a teacher of young minds.*

Help me to instill in my students

> *the ways of your wisdom;*
>
> *the depths of your understanding;*
>
> *the peace of your counsel;*
>
> *the power of your fortitude;*
>
> *the wonder of your knowledge;*
>
> *the joy of your piety;*
>
> *and the fire of your divine love.*

Let me never forget that my efforts
are to the greater honor and glory
of God—always.

Amen.

My Morning Prayer

O, my God, thank you.

Through your grace and goodness,

I hold the gift of a new day.

In your name,

> *I will respect its routines,*
>
> *welcome its surprises,*
>
> *and explore your presence in every minute.*

For somewhere in the gift of this day, O Lord,

you will teach me

that which I will teach another.

Amen.

Prayer Before Planning a Lesson

Some prayers, God, don't seem to have a beginning. Rather, we just realize at some point that we've been praying all along. This is one of those prayers.

I've been thinking about planning my lesson for days—and now I realize that my thinking has also been prayer. I've not asked, specifically, for your help. I've not invoked the holy name of your Son, Jesus. And I've not called on the guidance of your Holy Spirit. But in thinking about planning this lesson, I've certainly lifted my heart and mind to you—and that, indeed, is prayer. Now, I am specific.

Help me, God.
In the name of your Son, Jesus,
I ask for the guidance of your Holy Spirit.
Hear my prayer.
Amen.

Lesson Plan Blessing

Good and Gracious God,

I always enjoy this moment of accomplishment, when my lesson plan is complete. As always, my efforts have been inspired by your Spirit. I am grateful.

In the ancient tradition of our Church, I lay my hands on this lesson and ask that you bless it and make it worthy of my students' attentions. Let it teach them and inspire them—perhaps even entertain them. Most of all, may this lesson be for them an encounter with your Son, Jesus.

Amen.

Prayer Before Class

Almighty God and Father,

students will begin to arrive soon.

Open wide my spiritual arms

as I welcome and embrace them.

Bless this space,

> *so that the goodness of your truth*
>
> *may be shared.*

Bless this time,

> *so that the power of your love*
>
> *may be discovered.*

And bless me, Lord,

> *that I may share your Good News*
>
> *with joy and confidence.*

Amen.

Prayer for My Students

They are children, Dear God,

your children, our children.

Their faith and hope today

will shape their lives tomorrow.

Stir in them a longing

    to hear the Good News,

    to celebrate the wonder of life,

    and to know your Son as Friend.

I offer this prayerful plea, Dear God,

in the name of your Child, Jesus.

                            Amen.

Prayer for Special Needs of a Student

I take this quiet moment with you, Lord, to hold in prayer your precious child, (name the child).

You know this child's needs even better than those of us who care for and love her/him. Let this young soul know of your secure love and gentle presence. Send your angels to hover 'round (name the child), and to guide and (add a word that best suits the situation) her/him.

And instill in me the knowledge and courage of your Holy Spirit to be there for her/him in ways that are most caring and supportive. Amen.

Prayer for Special Classroom Needs

Gentle Jesus,

Your heart is especially gentle toward those in need—and my class is in need. (Bring to mind your specific need.)

I put myself in the service of your will to have this need met. Guide and advise me in exploring all resources and opportunities that will be helpful.

I know you hear my plea, Jesus. I trust in your care, and I trust in your miracles. *Amen.*

Prayer for My Students' Families

Gracious God, Source of Life,

You have planted the goodness of my students in the gardens of their families. Make that family soil rich in the virtues of faith, hope, and charity. Moisten it with the baptismal waters of your saving grace, and turn it with the plow of peace. Warm it with the radiance of your Son, Jesus, and sprinkle it with an abundance of your Holy Spirit. Pull from it the weeds of greed and anger, and protect it from the savage winds of indifference.

Let my students and their families grow deep roots of faith in community, and bloom in profusion in your eternal Kingdom. *Amen.*

Prayer with My Students

(Help your students memorize this simple litany.)

In the name of the Father,
and of the Son,
and of the Holy Spirit.

Amen.

Touch our hearts, Lord …
R. Be with us.
Let us learn, Lord …
R. Be with us.
Lift our minds, Lord …
R. Be with us.
Show the way, Lord …
R. Be with us.
Move our hearts, Lord …
R. Be with us.
Teach us love, Lord …
R. Be with us.

In the name of the Father,
and of the Son,
and of the Holy Spirit.

Amen.

Prayer After Class

Here it is, Lord, that special "class-is-over" feeling.

> *Maybe it's fatigue.*
> *Maybe it's relief.*
> *Maybe it's satisfaction.*
> *Maybe it's prayer.*

I'm not sure. But it's a familiar feeling.

In this class-is-over time, I hear you tell me your parable about the mustard seed. "From one tiny seed," you tell me, "grows the largest of plants that puts forth large branches, where the birds can dwell in its shade." I trust in your grace to bring forth an abundant harvest from the tiny seeds of faith and love that I plant in your name.

And Lord, when the next class is over, tell me again about the mustard seed. Amen.

Prayer of Gratitude

Gracious God,

Something worked—and it worked well. Thank you for that! It was good and it was holy and it was yours.

Oh sure, I am enjoying a small measure of credit for this success. After all, you created the human heart to know this kind of gleeful satisfaction. But I know beyond any doubt that your grace was fully present there and then—and is, still. Receive my humble "thank you," Gracious God!

Now I know you will excuse me, God, as I rush off in my excitement, like your dear child Mary Magdalene, to tell others about this wonderful something that worked! Amen.

Prayer to Share with Other Catechists

Lord, we gather with a common heritage—our faith.

We gather with a common purpose—to teach that faith.

As a small faith community, we pray for our students and ask that you show us how best to instruct them and share the faith with them.

We pray for our students' parents and ask that you show us how best to support them in their role as the primary educators of their children.

And we pray for the needs of all of us gathered here. (Pause.) Help us to show one another how to live faithfully, hope joyfully, and love courageously.

Amen.

Prayer for Our Faith Formation Team

Loving Jesus,

We are not Scripture scholars, theologians, or Church historians. Rather, we are a ragged band of your humble disciples.

Although we have countless other responsibilities—some of them pretty burdensome—each of us said "yes" to being part of our parish faith formation team.

You told your disciples to carry the Good News to the ends of the earth. Well, our "ends of the earth" are right here, right now.

Let us find among ourselves and in one another a very special community of faith—so that our simple efforts to preach the Good News of the Kingdom may truly, someday, reach the ends of the earth.

Amen.

Prayer for Our Religious Education Program

The success of our religious education program is in your keeping, Lord.

The work of our hearts and hands can organize and implement classes, service projects, sacrament prep programs, prayer services, Masses with children, retreats, and parish catechesis events. But only you, Lord, can breathe into these efforts the enduring life of your Spirit.

May our religious education program always be in you, of you, and for you. *Amen.*

Prayer for Our Parish

Almighty God,

This parish is our spiritual home and our spiritual family.

> *Here we introduce our newborns and ask for the Baptism of eternal life.*
>
> *Here we learn about and confirm our faith, confess our sins, celebrate our love, commit our lives to service, bless our sick and aging, and bury our dead.*
>
> *Here we know our oneness in the blessing, breaking, and sharing of the Body and Blood of your Son, Jesus.*

Bless our parish, God. May a mixture of charity, mercy, and forgiveness be the mortar that holds secure our foundations of faith. *Amen.*

Prayer When I'm Lacking Confidence

God, the challenges of being a catechist are demanding, so I need to be confident. But I don't always feel confident—like right now. I start thinking about the vast fields of Scripture, dogma, and Church history—so much of which I know so little. How is it that I think I can teach others?

So I pray. Help me to remember that knowledge is not the most important measure of my ability to teach and preach your word. First and foremost, I need love. Steady my timid soul, God, in a secure love of you and of my faith. Amen.

Prayer When I'm Feeling Unappreciated

Just hear me out, God—just for a minute.

It's a fact. I'm feeling unappreciated. Here I am, toiling away in the vineyard, where the laborers are few. I'm putting yeast in the dough. I'm tending the sheep. I'm preparing a banquet. I'm sowing the seed. I'm being the good steward, the good Samaritan, and the salt of the Earth—all rolled into one. I'm a Christ-bearer … but does anyone care?

Just a simple "Thank you" would be nice. "We appreciate all you do" would be even better. (Pause. Take a deep breath. Take another deep breath. Smile. Say "Amen" out loud.)

Prayer When I'm Feeling Burnout

God, I feel spent. That delicious beginning-of-the-learning-year energy has slipped away, leaving me listless. My spirit is heavy and my enthusiasm is artificial. At times, even my smile is forced.

Where is that Gospel vigor, God, that carried me along so effortlessly months ago? Where is that sense of myself as a disciple carrying out a sacred mission entrusted to your Church? And adding to my weariness is embarrassment that I feel this way at all.

I will do what I can for myself, God, but I leave the rest to you. Give me a Pentecost that transforms this lifeless feeling into renewed vitality and fresh resolve—for the good of my students, for my own good, and for the good of all the Church. Amen.

A Catechist's Divine Praises

Blessed be you, Almighty God.

> *Blessed be your most sacred word.*

Blessed be you, God's Only Son.

> *Blessed be your redeeming grace.*

Blessed be you, O Holy Spirit.

> *Blessed be your abiding love.*

Blessed be these soul-treasured truths.

> *Blessed be our eternal life.*

Blessed be this firm gift of faith.

> *Blessed be this my call to share it.*